HAL•LEONARD
INSTRUMENTAL PLAY-ALONG

TENOR SAX

Disney Greats

How To Use The CD Accompaniment:
A melody cue appears on the right channel only. If your CD player has a balance adjustment, you can adjust the volume of the melody by turning down the right channel.

ISBN 978-0-634-08542-0

HAL•LEONARD®
CORPORATION

7777 W. BLUEMOUND RD. P.O. BOX 13819 MILWAUKEE, WI 53213

Visit Hal Leonard Online at
www.halleonard.com

Disney Greats
CONTENTS

◆ ARABIAN NIGHTS

from Walt Disney's ALADDIN

TENOR SAX

Lyrics by HOWARD ASHMAN
Music by ALAN MENKEN

Moderately bright

❷ THE BARE NECESSITIES

from Walt Disney's THE JUNGLE BOOK

Words and Music by
TERRY GILKYSON

TENOR SAX

❸ A CHANGE IN ME

from Walt Disney's BEAUTY AND THE BEAST: THE BROADWAY MUSICAL

TENOR SAX

Words by TIM RICE
Music by ALAN MENKEN

◆ HAWAIIAN ROLLER COASTER RIDE

from Walt Disney's LILO & STITCH

TENOR SAX

Words and Music by ALAN SILVESTRI
and MARK KEALI'I HO'OMALU

❺ HONOR TO US ALL

from Walt Disney Pictures' MULAN

TENOR SAX

Music by MATTHEW WILDER
Lyrics by DAVID ZIPPEL

❻ I'M STILL HERE
(Jim's Theme)
from Walt Disney's TREASURE PLANET

TENOR SAX

Words and Music by
JOHN RZEZNIK

7 IT'S A SMALL WORLD

from "IT'S A SMALL WORLD" at Disneyland Park and Magic Kingdom Park

TENOR SAX

Words and Music by RICHARD M. SHERMAN
and ROBERT B. SHERMAN

◆9 THE MEDALLION CALLS

from Walt Disney Pictures' PIRATES OF THE CARIBBEAN: THE CURSE OF THE BLACK PEARL

TENOR SAX

Music by KLAUS BADELT

◆8 LOOK THROUGH MY EYES

from Walt Disney Pictures' BROTHER BEAR

TENOR SAX

Words and Music by
PHIL COLLINS

PROMISE

from MILLENNIUM CELEBRATION at Epcot

TENOR SAX

Music by GAVIN GREENAWAY
Words by DON DORSEY

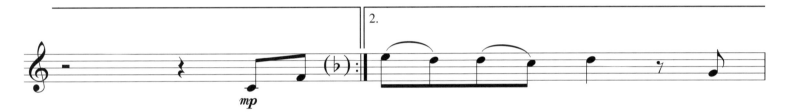

THE SIAMESE CAT SONG

from Walt Disney's LADY AND THE TRAMP

TENOR SAX

Words and Music by PEGGY LEE
and SONNY BURKE

SUPERCALIFRAGILISTICEXPIALIDOCIOUS

from Walt Disney's MARY POPPINS

TENOR SAX

Words and Music by RICHARD M. SHERMAN
and ROBERT B. SHERMAN

⑬ TWO WORLDS

from Walt Disney Pictures' TARZAN™

TENOR SAX

Words and Music by
PHIL COLLINS

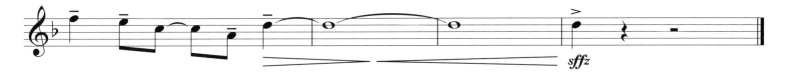

⟨14⟩ WHERE THE DREAM TAKES YOU

from Walt Disney Pictures' ATLANTIS: THE LOST EMPIRE

TENOR SAX

Lyrics by DIANE WARREN
Music by DIANE WARREN and JAMES NEWTON HOWARD

⬥15 YO HO
(A Pirate's Life for Me)
from PIRATES OF THE CARIBBEAN at Disneyland Park and Magic Kingdom Park

TENOR SAX

Words by XAVIER ATENCIO
Music by GEORGE BRUNS

In a robust manner